F

FAST

40 YARD DASH

Attain Football Speed Dominance using
11 Olympic-Sprinter Running Mechanics

Dedication

MJ DeMarco, I know you hate the spotlight, but I'm still going to shine it on you because credit needs to go where credit is due: Were it not for your work, truly, I never would have completed this book. It's with deep gratitude that I dedicate this work to you.

Thanks

I could never list all of the people who are deserving of an enormous "THANK YOU" for their roles in my life that led to the creation of this book. Please know that I have so much gratitude to all of my supporters, mentors, friends, family, co-workers, and fans.

I'd like to specifically express gratitude to Colin Kibler, Geri Kibler, Tracy Coats, Jacqueline Pelsey, Mike Caza, and my father. Colin, you're a great friend and the world would do well to have more people like you (he's also a hilarious comedian—check out one of his shows next time you're in Chicago). Geri, you're a wonderful human being. Tracy, you got me started and that was just what I needed. Jacqueline, you're a kind-hearted, intelligent person who truly desires to use your gifts to help others. Mike, you've taught me so much about the art of sprinting, and for that I'm grateful. And dad, thank you for teaching me the basics of exercising when I was a kid.

Thank you!

Read This First

Before diving in, there are four quick pieces of information you need to know. First, this book contains no pictures. However, YouTube videos of Olympic sprinters are referenced to give you a visual of each of the running mechanics discussed. Specifically, those videos are "Asafa Powell Start" by Daniel Ryan and "Christian Coleman Fastest 40 Yard Dash Ever!" by Sports Vidz (a complete reference of both videos is found in Part I of this book). These will be your visual aids to go along with the descriptions of each of the Olympic Sprinter Running Mechanics (OSRMs).

Second, as a purchaser of this book you get one discounted video analysis of your 40 yard dash sprint start. You can find the information pertinent to this at the end of the book.

Third, it's obvious that this book has been written specifically for football players. In a sport where just fractions of a second can be the difference-maker in earning thousands of dollars in athletic scholarships or earning a spot on the varsity squad, sprinting speed is pinnacle. However, the running techniques in this book also apply to other sports requiring sprinting speed. A few of those other sports include, but are not limited to, track and field, basketball, baseball, soccer, rugby, lacrosse, and softball.

Lastly, although this has been written as if I'm having a conversation with football players, the information found here is also useful for coaches and parents who work with football players. Coaches, please note that I may speak of certain unhelpful ways of training which many coaches utilize. I'm not speaking directly to you. Remember, I'm writing this *to* athletes and *for* athletes. The information in this book is helpful for coaches, but it wasn't written *to* coaches. We've all had the experience of working with a coach who was difficult and ineffective. When I speak about such coaches in this book, I'm doing so for the purpose of supporting and encouraging the *athletes* out there who find themselves in such an unfortunate situation. If you are a coach and are reading this book, clearly you're different than that type of coach, and therefore you know that I am not speaking about you when I offer athletes guidance in working with difficult coaches.

Table of Contents

I. Mental Preparation 5

II. The 3 Phases of the 40 Yard Dash 27

1. 3-Point Stance Phase 32

2. Drive Phase 42

3. Upright Running Phase 70

4. Summary 87

III. Mindset 92

IV. 6 Week Program 98

Part I
Mental Preparation

"Nic, I want to thank you for your expertise in helping me get off the line fast. I use these techniques today in my professional NFL career."
-Pierre Garcon, NFL Wide Receiver

Genetics vs. Intelligent Effort

It takes a trained eye to understand the technical movements Olympic sprinters utilize during a race. To most onlookers, they simply see a bunch of strong, fit-looking athletes running fast. Little do they know that these sprinters are using highly specific running mechanics to get the most out of their speed potential.

I didn't learn these techniques until my second year as a collegiate athlete. I wish I would have known the Olympic Sprinter Running Mechanics (**OSRM**s) contained in this book as a high school athlete. In high school, I fell short of making the finals at the state meet as a sprinter. Twice. Had I practiced and understood these techniques, I would have been an all-state sprinter in high school. Instead, I had to wait a few years. As a freshman in college, I experienced a slump year due to poor training, followed by an average year as a sophomore. It wasn't until my third year in college, junior year, that I became an all-American sprinter after having the opportunity to apply the Olympic Sprinter Running Mechanics you will find in this book. Had I sought answers sooner, I could have started to change the trajectory of my athletic career much earlier. This book will empower you to begin *now*, rather than waiting like I did.

Sprinting speed, and thereby your 40 yard dash speed, can be broken down into two components: 1) Power and 2) Technique. If you don't improve your power whatsoever, improved technique can still make you faster because it makes the *most* out of the power you currently possess. Many athletes are nowhere near their 40 yard dash potential due to sloppy technique.

In college, I competed on the track team as a sprinter, and one of my competitors comes to mind. He was a specimen of power: Strong and explosive with well-developed, ripped muscles. But, wow, was his technique awful. And that slowed him down tremendously. His legs flailed and his arm action moved side-to-side instead of front to back. He was dispersing his power in directions that were not useful for covering a straight line as fast as possible.

Although he was outputting more overall power than the other athletes on the track, the *direction* of his power output was unfocused. Of course, if you were to run 40 yards in a flailing, zigzag fashion, you'll run a slower time than if you were to run straight ahead. In the same way, if your limbs are outputting power in all kinds of crazy angles, your power will be dispersed in directions other than straight ahead. *Straight ahead* is the direction you want to focus your power output so as to cover 40 yards as fast as possible.

From my freshman eyes, the competitor I described was untouchable. He was this muscular, strong, larger-than-life guy who I couldn't come close to competing against. However, with consistent training, I crept up on him. Eventually, after two years of dedicated, focused training, he was of no concern to me in competition. He was naturally more powerful than I was, but I sought out the most advanced, intelligent sprinting techniques possible. Had my competitor done the same, I have no doubt he would have beaten me. But, like so many other talented athletes, his form stayed the same over the duration of his collegiate career, whereas mine constantly evolved for the better.

With dedicated, focused training, you can outperform athletes with superior genetics.

What is Required of You

Before diving in, you should know that there are no pictures in this book. You'll have to read the descriptions of the mechanics Olympic sprinters use, and then focus your mind to understand and apply the techniques to your 40 yard dash. This is a good thing, and I'm going to tell you why.

Now, most athletes will lament the fact that mining the gold from this book requires effort on their part. But not you. With a high barrier of entry, only the most serious, dedicated athletes with an improve-at-all-costs attitude will apply the techniques in this book, thereby creating a rare, significant edge over the other athletes in their category.

Recently, I trained an 8th grader who was running track (100m dash) for the first time while also preparing for the upcoming football season. He took the techniques I taught him to heart, practicing them and visualizing them during his spare moments. "Sometimes, while I'm walking, I'll just bust out into Triple Extension." (Triple

Extension is one of the techniques you'll learn in this book). Unsurprisingly, he had the best sprint start in his region. He wasn't the most muscular or genetically gifted athlete, but as a result of his dedication to mastering the same mechanical running techniques you will find in this book, 11 Olympic Sprinter Running Mechanics (OSRM), he gave himself a significant, rare edge. After all, how many 8th graders are willing to dedicate themselves to mastering such a skill? He didn't lament the fact that it took "hard work" to learn the mechanics; instead, he energetically practiced them, ultimately leading to an explosive sprint start which was noticed by both fans and coaches.

Now that I've scared away most readers with the fact that there are no pictures in this book, consider this: As an athlete, I was never a huge fan of pictures in a book because they didn't tell the entire story. I had the same opinion about videos because, inevitably, a video would show a top-notch athlete performing a movement requiring a high degree of skill. The video would then be accompanied by some simplistic, unhelpful explanation.

For example, as a middle schooler, I was into BMX dirt jumping. I purchased a video made by professional BMX dirt jumpers thinking,

"Awesome! They're going to teach me how to do high-difficulty moves!" (or something to that extent--I doubt I used the term "high-difficulty"). I was pumped. So, the video showed the pro doing one of the moves I wanted to learn, a 360 X-Up. "Wow, looks awesome. Can't wait for the explanation."

Here's the explanation they gave: Hit the jump. Turn your body in the direction you want to spin while simultaneously crossing your arms. Land smoothly, and ride away."

Uh, I'm sorry, "ride away"? The descriptions were utterly pitiful. Sure, I could watch them perform the movement on the video, but what about the intricate understanding of BMX biomechanics? You don't just "turn your body, land, and ride away." *There are specific sub-movements that create the overall movement.* Sub-movements that, if you're a novice with an untrained eye, you wouldn't, _couldn't_, notice. Teach me *how* to perform the moves. Don't give me some over-simplified, unhelpful explanation. The video was a waste of money.

In this book, I'm not going to tell you things like, "Just drive off the ground, stay low, and run through the line." But hey, that's the type of 40 yard dash description you'll get on tons of YouTube videos. "Just stay low for about 20 meters. Pump your arms." Wow, so helpful. You need to know *how* to stay low. What are the subtle sub-movements Olympic sprinters are using to create the big picture of sprinting fast? In case it's unclear: There are definite, concrete techniques Olympic sprinters utilize to maximize their sprinting speed which are not observable through an untrained eye. This book will discuss, in detail, 11 Olympic Sprinter Running Mechanics (OSRM).

Learning to apply these speed mechanics of Olympic sprinters for the purpose of maximizing your speed requires an understanding of body angles and movements. You need the detailed description about how to make those specific movements happen, not some video of an athlete doing the movement with no explanation about how to actually arrive at the point of being capable of performing that movement yourself.

In other words, you're going to be required to engage your mind. "Aw man, I'm already in school and I don't want to do much more thinking than I'm already doing." That's fine, but another athlete, maybe your competitor from another team, or teammate who is shooting for the same starting position as you on the varsity lineup, *will* do the work you won't do. Now he's got an edge over you. Applying the techniques in this book will absolutely be worth it for you as an athlete, especially if you're looking to play in college (or beyond) or secure a starting position on the high school varsity team. Yes, you'll need to focus, visualizing and feeling out the movements as you read the descriptions. Visualize the descriptions and perform them in your backyard or living room before taking them to the turf.

By the way, Visualization is OSRM #1, which we'll get to after the following section.

Keep in Mind

Remember, learning the sprinting mechanics Olympic sprinters use is no easy task. It will require focus and dedication. There will be days when you don't want to train, but train anyway. That's what it takes. If you apply the techniques in this book, you'll see a significant improvement in your 40 yard dash speed. But I'm not going to play games with you and say it's going to be an effortless process. However, I will say this: If you are committed to utilizing the techniques in this book, you will stand out in your position category. You'll be the noticeable lineman who explodes off the line faster than the majority of other linemen. You'll be the running back who covers 10 yards faster than the others. Coaches, scouts, and teammates will notice the change in you. Again, that is only if you *apply* the information in this book. Reading it alone will not get you there.

As a collegiate sprinter, I had the fastest 40 in the nation. At the indoor track and field nationals, I placed 3rd in the short sprint (55m dash); however, at the 40 yard mark, I was in first place. Explosiveness off the line is what a faster 40 is all about. Also, considering that I was ranked about 1000th in the nation during my first season as a collegiate sprinter (didn't qualify for nationals), jumping to 3rd was a hefty improvement. I didn't miss training days. Didn't overlook details. Didn't say, "I'll do this portion of the workout, but not that portion." Ate well, and made sure I was getting enough sleep. This is the way of Olympic sprinters. They not only put in the time, but they also do so with a great amount of focus.

You do have what it takes. Whether you'll *do* what it takes is up to you. Laid before you, this very moment, is the opportunity to drastically improve your 40 yard dash speed. Are you one of the athletes who wants it so **badly** you can literally feel it coursing through your veins? Remember, it's in you, but will you use your ability or go the route of laziness and video games like so many other athletes who have wasted their talent? I hope you'll choose to maximize your potential, leaving no room for regrets or a "what-if?" when your competitive days are over.

Visualization

Obviously, Visualization is not a physically executed running mechanic. However, elite sprinters use it so often as a means to ingrain proper sprint mechanics into their bodies, this technique deserves a place among the physical sprinting mechanics.

Check this out: Scientifically, we know that the same nerves are activated when *visualizing* a movement as when physically performing that movement. Yes, it's true. Studies using Olympic athletes attached electrodes to them and measured brain activation when visualizing their event (as opposed to physically performing their event). What scientists discovered is that the same nerves were activated in the body during Visualization as during physically performing the event. With that in mind, **visualize sprinting techniques before physically performing them**. Feel them out in your mind. See yourself performing the techniques described in this book. If a technique calls for complete extension of your push off leg, first visualize yourself completely extending the leg as you powerfully drive off the ground.

The difference between Visualization and watching a premade video involves the concept of active engagement vs. passive engagement. When visualizing a described movement, you must engage your mind. Being in an engaged-mind state ingrains the movement into your nervous system. On the other hand, watching a premade video is passive. It's there, you look at it, maybe get some intellectual understanding, but nothing shifts in your neuromuscular system. This is why Olympic sprinters use Visualization— because it puts them in a state of active engagement, which has a positive effect on their neuromuscular system. In other words, an athlete's body is more likely to automatically perform a movement, without thinking about it, as a result of Visualization.

With that said, be aware that I am going to refer you to some YouTube videos of sprinters who brilliantly display the techniques described in this book. It won't be enough to simply watch the video. You must read the description of the movement, then watch the video, then *reread* the description, then visualize yourself performing the motion. If that sounds like a lot of work, that's because it is. A lot of athletes want to get better, but not many athletes are willing to do the work required to get better.

As you utilize this book, use the process described above. Here it is, broken down for you:

- First, read the technique description.
- Next, watch the YouTube video.
- Then, reread the description.
- Finally, visualize yourself performing the movement.

Although four action steps may seem like a lot, it actually saves you time. You're going to spend more time fiddling with your technique if you take it directly from reading to the turf. On the other hand, if you first take the time to ingrain the mechanics into your mind, you will save yourself time when practicing on the field.

Become friends with this process, as it will aid in ingraining the Olympic Sprinter Running Mechanics into your neuromuscular system. "Neuro" implies brain activity, while "muscular" implies the usage of muscles. *Movement* is a result of brain activity *plus* muscular activation. If you want to fine tune your 40 yard dash sprinting technique, first practice the "neuro" component, then the physical movement component.

The Importance of Technique

The purpose of this book is to teach you the sprinting techniques that will result in the fastest 40 yard dash you can possibly run, given your current strength and power capabilities. There are many excellent Olympic training methods to increase your power, thus improving your 40 yard dash speed; however, that is outside the scope of this little book.

The purpose of improved sprinting technique is to make you run faster times. Period. The reason Olympic sprinters put so much effort into refining their technique is because they know that more efficient technique will allow them to make the *most* out of their athletic ability.

Consider the athlete who steps side-to-side along the turf as he drives out of the 3-point stance vs. stepping straight ahead. The athlete who steps side-to-side is going to make less forward progress than he potentially could have had he stepped straight ahead. The difference isn't much when considering just one individual step. Cumulatively, however, over the course of the entire 40 yard dash, the loss of forward-progress with each step adds up with each stride, leading to overall slower times.

As a collegiate track and field athlete, I had the honor of training like an Olympic sprinter because I came into contact with a coach who possessed this rare knowledge. He was a world-class athlete who traveled the world competing. Along the way, he had the opportunity to work with some of the best sprint coaches in history, as well as train side-by-side with some of the best sprinters in history (I know, I know, you want names. I'll elaborate on this more later). As a result of refining my technique, I consistently blew my competition out of the water in terms of the sprint start. I could devastate sprinters over 40 yards who had much higher top speeds than I did and subsequently beat me over 100 meters. In football, however, 100 meter speed truly does not matter (except in rare cases). *Explosiveness* off the line is what matters 99% of the time. Don't worry yourself so much with top speed; to be a more valuable football player, concern yourself with training for explosiveness off the line.

The athletes I've trained have experienced the same results in their sprint starts as I did. Applying the Olympic Sprinter Running

Mechanics in this book will give you a huge edge over your competition, primarily because proper coaching application of what you'll find here is rare. For example, you can search YouTube and find some of the top sprinters in the world explaining sprint start technique. #LOL. They can execute the technique for themselves; however, they lack the analytical skills to break it down in terms anybody can apply. It's like my BMX video all over again (mentioned earlier). "Have tunnel vision. Swing your arms hard." I'm sure they think they are being helpful, but again, the "how" is much too generalized for an athlete to apply in a meaningful way, as the sub-movements are not described. In addition, a large number of coaches struggle to ingrain these techniques into their athletes (but not you, as you are clearly proactive as shown by reading this book). Reason being, they haven't had the blended experience of both learning from a world-class coach and applying the techniques themselves. A coach may "get" the concepts insofar as he can intellectually grasp them, but an intellectual understanding can never be as powerful as experience combined with intellectual understanding. The elite sprinters posting on YouTube have the experience but lack the intellectual skills to communicate their experience. Most coaches have the intellectual understanding but lack the personal experience as an athlete. This book will blend my personal experience as an athlete with intellectual understanding, giving you the best of both worlds.

I've been coaching sprint starts for a long time at all levels, from the middle school level to the NFL level, and I know the application of what you'll learn here *will make you sprint faster*.

As previously mentioned, I will reference a couple of YouTube videos within this book. If you don't have internet access at home, that's okay. Make a note to yourself and then search for the videos at the public library or at school.

2-Step Success Process

Successfully applying what you learn in this little book is a 2-step process. Step #1 is to focus on what you read. This idea of focusing on what you read was already mentioned, but it's important enough to be repeated. Some of the concepts are going to be new to you. Utilize your brainpower to focus on what you're reading. If you don't think you're smart enough or somehow lack brainpower, I'm telling you right now that such a belief is hogwash. If you've been made to feel dumb by your parents, siblings, teachers, or classmates, understand that those people are just placing their own insecurities onto you. Never allow someone to make you feel intellectually incapable. If they were happy, confident people, they wouldn't want to make anyone feel dumb. So, if you believe you somehow lack the ability to understand the concepts in this book, throw that aside immediately. It's not true! If you can read and if you can visualize, you can understand these concepts, and therefore run a faster 40 yard dash.

Your intellect is like a muscle. An untrained muscle can't lift much weight. It's not that the person is "incapable," it's that they're *untrained*. Just because you haven't exercised your intellect doesn't mean you're "incapable." Not at all. It simply means you need to practice applying your intellect. It's unlikely that most other athletes will take this seriously. All the better, as this gives you an edge over them. As you read, stop periodically to try the motion. Whether it's in your living room at home or in front of the mirror at the gym doesn't matter, just practice the motions while visualizing them in your mind (more on this in a minute). Step #1 requires a focused effort on your part. Simply reading about these techniques one time is not going to magically implant them into your neuromuscular system.

Step #2 is to practice the techniques. Olympic sprinters practice these techniques year-round, day in, day out. As a result, their bodies perform the movements subconsciously. You definitely don't want to be thinking about these techniques when it's game time or 40 testing time. Thinking tightens the body, which slows you down. The key to a stellar 3-point start is to practice the mechanics so much your body will perform the movements subconsciously, like an app running in the background. Your job is to stay loose and just run.

Do not fool yourself into thinking that a few practice sessions will do the trick. Studies vary in terms of the number of repetitions it takes to ingrain a movement into your body. It depends on the complexity of the movement. Here's what I suggest as a starting point: Practice the movements 10x a day for six weeks. I've outlined a 6-week program for you in Part IV. After that, see where you're at. This is no joke. Varsity starting positions and college scholarships are *out there for the taking*, but the athlete who trains in a consistent, focused manner is going to have an edge over athletes who train haphazardly.

Most athletes your age are not willing to put in the work it takes to make a significant improvement. They'll say things like, "I'm not fast enough to play in college," or "I'm not big enough to play in college." They make these comments as if they aren't capable of getting faster or bigger.

I could have said, "I'm not fast enough to compete at nationals." After a horrible freshman season, it sure seemed that way, but I didn't see myself as not fast enough, even though I wasn't close to making nationals as a freshman. Instead, I said, "What's it going to take to make myself fast enough to compete at nationals?" Then, I took daily action and put in the work. Sick, tired, busy...none of that mattered. When out of town, I found a gym in the area I was visiting. On holidays when the training facilities were closed, I adjusted my training for that day, never using holiday hours or snow as an excuse not to train. Over the years, "adjusting" my training has meant many things. To name just a few:

- I've done squats with a person on my shoulders when barbells weren't available.

- I've put on cleats and ran hills in the snow when the indoor track wasn't open over the holidays.
- I've done plyometric pushups on a stack of books when medicine balls weren't available.
- I've jumped the fence of a locked stadium around 10:00 p.m. at night during exam week in college. If you're unfamiliar with college exam weeks, they throw off your entire schedule and eat up your entire day. I don't suggest doing illegal or dangerous things like this, but it highlights the fact that I refused to let there be an excuse not to train.

It's never a matter of "I can't do it today" rather, it's a matter of how creative you're willing to be. Get creative and look for ways to still train even when -- no, *especially when* -- your current environmental conditions aren't ideal.

Do you think the majority of your competition is putting cleats on and running in the snow? Do you think your competition is training on the holidays? Maybe 1/1000 athletes. Who do you want to be, the **one** or the other 999?

Know that I didn't relay the above experiences to you for the purpose of tooting my own horn. My hope is that it'll light a fire under you. You *can* be faster. It will, however, require a focused effort on your part, especially when it comes to making time to practice the Olympic Sprinter Running Mechanics in this book.

Improvement, Not Perfection

As you read this book, do not attempt to make your sprinting form perfect. Simply have a goal of improving upon it each day. The risk in shooting for perfection is that you'll suffer paralysis by analysis. Each time you get up to the line to perform a rep, you'll be psyching yourself out over making the sprint perfect. Don't make perfection a priority; make *improvement* your priority. With an Improvement Mindset you *will* sprint faster, but without the stress and anxiety of over-analysis.

Now your mind is in the right place, so let's get after it.

Part II

The 3 Phases of the 40 Yard Dash

At this point, enough has been said about what it's going to take for you to get better, so let's dive in.

The 40 yard dash consists of three primary phases. Those three phases are:

1. 3-Point Stance Phase
2. Drive Phase
3. Upright Running Phase

Here's what's about to happen: I'm going to breakdown, in detail, each of the three phases. Using the forest vs. trees analogy, you're about to zoom in and take a close look at each of the individual trees within the larger forest. Then, after detailing each of the three phases of the 40 yard dash, I'm going to zoom back out and put it all together for you in a fluid, big picture fashion.

OSRM Organization

Each **OSRM** (Olympic Sprinter Running Mechanic[s]) will be categorized within a specific phase of the 40 yard dash. For example, within the 3-Point Stance Phase, there are three OSRMs to be discussed which apply to that specific phase.

As you can see, each OSRM is not given a number 1-11 (there are 11 total). The reason why is because I want you to associate each OSRM with the phase of the 40 yard dash it belongs to. This way, when you're practicing any one of the phases, you can remind yourself, "Okay, I'm working on my Drive Phase. *Within* the Drive Phase, there are four OSRMs I need to work on." Categorizing each OSRM within the phase it belongs to allows you to specifically focus on that portion of the 40 (remember the importance of sub-movements), without having to remember which OSRM numbers from 1-11 apply to each phase. "There are three OSRMs in the Upright Running Phase" is much easier to draw upon than "OSRM #s 9, 10, and 11 apply to the Upright Running Phase, while #s 5, 6, 7, and 8 apply to the Drive Phase, and so on." Below, you'll find a breakdown of the OSRMs within each phase of the 40 yard dash.

\# OSRMs per phase of the 40 yard dash:

Visualization: 1 OSRM
1.   Visualization

3-Point Stance Phase: 3 OSRMs
1.   Hip Height
2.   Elongated Torso
3.   Ball of the Foot

Drive Phase: 4 OSRMs
1.   Triple Extension
2.   Up-and-Forward to Down-and-Back
3.   Elongated Torso
4.   Powerful Arm Action

Upright Running Phase: 3 OSRMs
1.   Loose Shoulders
2.   Elevated Torso
3.   Cyclical Leg Action

Let's take a look at the first phase.

3-Point Stance Phase

The 3-point stance sets the tone for the entire 40 yard dash. A sloppy 3-point stance will likely result in a sloppy first couple of steps. Many athletes stumble over the first couple of steps and start running after that. To maximize your 40 yard dash speed, you'll need to propel your body forward *explosively* from the get-go. No wasted steps.

Although you aren't actually running during the 3-Point Stance Phase, it is vital you don't overlook its importance. Body angles play a role in determining force capabilities. For example, it's easier to perform a dumbbell biceps curl when beginning with a bend in the elbow joint than when beginning from a completely locked (straightened) elbow joint. Leg pressing 400 lbs would be easier from a beginning position where your hip and knee joints are slightly more extended (closer to straight-legged) than from a completely scrunched beginning position (tightly bent legs). In the same way joint angles make a difference in the weight room, they also make a difference in your 3-point stance when preparing to explode off the line and complete a 40 yard dash.

3 Common Mistakes

There are 3 common mistakes athletes make in the 3-Point Stance Phase of the 40 yard dash. I am going to describe each mistake, along with the OSRM you'll need to apply to correct the mistake.

Before we begin, take note that when in your 3-Point Stance Phase, the opposite hand of the front foot is down on the turf, while the same hand of the front foot is cocked back. If your left foot is forward, your right hand is on the turf, and vice versa. The reason for this is it creates balance. If you place the same hand down as the front foot, your spine is now twisted and bent, reducing core stability. As you'll discover in OSRM #2 of the 3-Point Stance Phase, a sturdy core is a cornerstone of exploding off the line fast.

Mistake 1

Hips too Low

The number one mistake I see athletes make in the 3-Point Stance Phase is that their hips are too low. Of course, you don't want your hips *way* up in the air; however, you need enough Hip Height to allow the cycling leg (the leg that is *off* the ground at any point during sprinting) to move freely beneath the hips without restriction.

3-Point Stance Phase OSRM #1

Hip Height

Many athletes get themselves into a stance where their hips and shoulders are approximately level. This is too low concerning hip position. This brings us to **OSRM #1 of the 3-Point Stance Phase**: **When in the 3-point stance, raise your hips so they are slightly above shoulder level**, about 2-3". By providing a bit more airspace between the bottom of your hips and the ground, your rear leg (when in the 3-point stance) has more room to drive forward without restriction. A cramped cycling leg results in shortchanging the length of your step and therefore not making full use of your leg power. That is, you're more likely to have a short, choppy stride (read: weak, inefficient), as opposed to a completely extended, powerful stride.

Athletes and coaches tend to fixate upon their knee angle, as if the knee joint is a more powerful prime mover than the hip joint. It's not! Connecting to the knee joint are the quadriceps, hamstrings, calves, and tibialis anterior (shin) muscles. Connecting to the hip joint, on the other hand, are the glute muscles -- enough said. The glutes are the strongest prime movers in your body when it comes to sprinting speed.

Along with the glutes are the adductors, abductors, hip flexors, abdominals, obliques, and lower back muscles. In other words, your hips are command central when it comes to explosively driving out of your 40 yard dash stance. With that in mind, do not fixate on the angle of your knee joint, rather, focus on an appropriate Hip Height, which is 2-3" above shoulder level so as to provide enough room for the rear leg to drive forward beneath the hips, without restriction.

Mistake 2
Hunched Back

I cover this area in even more detail in the Drive Phase section of this book. However, it applies to the 3-Point Stance Phase as well. With that in mind, this will be brief.

3-Point Stance Phase OSRM #2
Elongated Torso

If your back is hunched while in the 3-Point Stance Phase, you will not transfer as much power as possible into the turf. A hunched back is not a *sturdy back*.

3-Point Stance Phase OSRM #2: An Elongated Torso is sturdy, because elongation automatically engages the core and will

therefore transfer more leg power into the turf, as opposed to dispersing your leg power in an undesirable way. With a forward rolling back, the instability of your spine causes leg power to dissipate, resulting in not propelling you forward with the highest amount of explosiveness possible.

To ingrain this concept into your body, try a brief exercise. Sit with your shoulders and head hunched forward. Notice the forward roll in your back. Now, lift your head and shoulders up *slowly*, straightening your posture. Finally, elevate your rib cage ever so slightly (don't overexaggerate). Notice how your posture gains another inch when you raise your rib cage. Apply this posture to your 3-Point Stance. The torso should definitively be elongated as opposed to hunched but elongated in a relaxed manner. In other words, don't bear down on your core as if you're constipated and trying to make yourself go to the bathroom. Simply elongate the torso without exerting too much effort. Refer to the Elongated Torso category in the Drive Phase section of this book to learn more about the mechanical benefits of an Elongated Torso.

Mistake 3

Standing on Your Tippy Toes

"Get on your toes" is a well-intentioned but misguided cue used by many coaches and athletes. As a result of hearing this over and over, athletes preparing to run a 40 yard dash are up on the toe of the lead leg (the push off leg). By default, being "up on the toes" extends the ankle joint, leaving less potential range of motion to create power as the athlete drives off the line.

3-Point Stance Phase OSRM #3

Ball of the Foot

3-Point Stance Phase OSRM #3: The ball of your foot should be in definite, firm contact with the ground during the 3-Point Stance Phase, bearing more weight than the toes. This means your heel is slightly closer to the ground than it would be if you were on your toes. Remember, as you lift your hips to ready your 3-point stance, keep the Ball of the Foot firmly planted on the ground. Ensure that you avoid the mistake of letting the ball of your foot lift off the ground as you raise your hips in preparation for exploding off the line.

Mechanically, why is it so important to drive through the Ball of the Foot as opposed to the toes? *First*, the Ball of the Foot is a more stable surface than your toes, which means it will transfer power into the ground more effectively than the more unstable toes.

Second, supporting your body's weight on the Ball of the Foot primarily engages the hip joint, whereas supporting the body's weight on your toes primarily engages the knee joint. As you learned earlier, the hip joint is capable of conjuring more power than the knee joint due to its association with the glute muscles. Therefore, engaging the hips will allow you to drive forward more explosively than relying on the knee joint.

Third, range of motion. Go ahead and pull your toes up toward the knee, then extend them down toward the ground. This is the range of motion being referred to in this context, specifically the range of motion of the ankle joint. Greater range of motion results in greater ability to produce force. If you are on your toes in the 3-point stance, the ankle will have less capability to produce a wide range of motion, and therefore less force will be created. However, by standing on the ball of your foot, the ankle will have a larger range of motion potential as you drive your body forward, and therefore result in more power production as you drive off the line.

One way to think about this is by jumping off of two feet. First, stand on your toes and jump up as high as you can. You're not allowed to lower the heals before jumping. Just stand up on your toes and jump. Now, stand with your heels just barely off the ground and jump, going from heals near the ground to completely extending your ankle joint as you leap.

Building on this concept, I've never witnessed a world-class athlete perform the vertical leap from standing on the toes. They are always in a stance where the heel is just barely raised from the ground, allowing the balls of the feet to bear the weight of the body. The sprint start is similar to a vertical leap. The only differences are that sprint starts are off of one foot instead of two feet and involve horizontal propulsion rather than vertical propulsion. With the vertical leap and the sprint start, the goals are the same: Move the body as explosively as possible.

Here's a summary of the Olympic Sprinter Running Mechanics involved in the 3-Point Stance Phase with a few easy-to-refer-to bullet points.

- **Hip Height**. Make sure your hips are high enough, 2-3" above shoulder height, allowing the rear leg to pull effortlessly through. Hips that are too low will cramp the rear leg as it cycles through.

- **Elongated Torso**. A forward rolling back dissipates power. An Elongated Torso, however, transfers power created by the legs into the turf. In turn, this explosively propels the body down the field.

- **Ball of the Foot**. Lower your heel slightly to plant the ball of your push off leg firmly on the turf. This will give you more range of motion plus more stability, ultimately leading to a more explosive sprint start.

Now that you have knowledge, it's time to practice. Practice your 3-Point Stance Phase. Unlike the other phases of the 40 yard dash, this is something you can do at home. Simply make a line out of tape, a ruler, or use a preexisting line in the carpeting or floor. Knowledge without application is useless. You won't breakout into a faster 40 yard dash only by having the intellectual knowledge of these concepts. You will, however, breakout into a faster 40 by *applying* these concepts.

Remember: Elite athletes commit themselves to taking action. Consistent action is what will give you the results you want. Adopt an action-based mindset. It goes something like this: *Now that I know these concepts, I'm going to practice them.* Simple, yet, it's what separates the **one** from the other 999.

Drive Phase

Allow me to tell you a bit more about my coaching lineage. My coaching mentor, Mike Caza, learned from a coach by the name of Dan Pfaff, and Dan Pfaff worked under Tom Tellez for a period of time. So, who are these people? Pfaff was the coach of 100m Olympic gold medalist Donovan Bailey. In 1996, Bailey set the world record in the 100m. Tom Tellez was the coach of Carl Lewis and Leroy Burrell. Between the years 1987 and 1994, Lewis and Burrell went back and forth a few times, taking turns setting and lowering the 100m world record. In short, Tellez worked with Pfaff, Pfaff worked with Caza, and Caza worked with me. I'm #4 in this line of coaches. My desire is to pass along world-class sprinting techniques to athletes who would otherwise not have access to them. Take it all in.

The 4 Keys to a
World-Class Drive Phase

The four technical keys to world-class sprint start technique are as follows:

Wait. Before I spell this out for you, are you ready to take it in? As mentioned earlier in this book, I'd rather not give this information to athletes who are just going to skim over it and never apply it. I've literally spent 1000s of hours learning and perfecting these technical concepts, in addition to perfecting the most effective ways of communicating these concepts to other athletes. These *are* the same techniques Olympic 100m dash sprinters use. Using these sprint mechanics is the best way to improve your 40 yard dash technique. For speed athletes, this stuff is a goldmine. I'm happy to share my goldmine but prefer to share it with those who will make good use of it.

My goal in writing this book is that by the time you finish, you will have taken to heart the concepts of applying and practicing these techniques. With that in mind, I am going to be repetitive. The reason I'm going to be repetitive is because I want to see you get faster and achieve your athletic goals, and the only way that will happen is if you apply and practice what you find here. So, when you see I've stated the importance of applying and practicing these techniques for the 100th time in this book, know that I'm doing it because I want to see you succeed.

In the second part of this book, I've outlined a detailed 6-week program to get you started. Like storing a treasure trove of rare gems in your basement and forgetting about them, simply reading about these sprint mechanics concepts will be of no benefit to you. You must visualize them, and then put them into physical practice. Now, let's get to that goldmine I promised you.

The four Drive Phase OSRMs are as follows:
1. Triple Extension
2. Up-and-Forward with Transition to Down-and-Back
3. Elongated Torso
4. Powerful Arm Action

Drive Phase OSRM #1
Triple Extension

The first time I properly applied Triple Extension in competition I shocked myself because I wasn't even thinking about it. Leading up to that day I had consistently practiced the technique for a long period of time but seemed to consistently fall short on race day. One day, my practice came to fruition. Without thinking about it, I exploded out of the blocks and found myself further ahead of the pack than usual. If you practice a technique enough, it will eventually become second nature and your body will do it without conscious thought.

I qualified for nationals for the first time on that day, a huge breakthrough for me, and it was the beginning of consistently sprinting faster than I was previously capable of achieving. Progress can take time, but the hard, dedicated work is worth it in the end. In addition, by ingraining these mechanics into your body through consistent practice you won't only improve your 40, you'll also sprint faster on the field.

Triple Extension refers to the extension of three joints. Those three joints are the a) *hip joint*, b) *knee joint*, and c) *ankle joint*. I've been coaching sprint starts for 12+ years, and most athletes do not triple extend when driving out of the 3-point stance. Not triple extending is a good way to slow yourself down. Properly executed Triple Extension, on the other hand, is a great technique for achieving breakout times in your 40.

We'll start with an example. Imagine an athlete who starts with the left leg forward when in the 3-point stance. The athlete pushes into the ground with the left leg to initiate the 40 yard dash sprint start. If the right foot touches down to the ground before the hip, knee, and ankle joints of the left leg (push off leg) are completely locked out, then this athlete <u>did</u> <u>not</u> triple extend. In other words, if there is any bend remaining in the push-off leg, Triple Extension did not occur. To properly visualize Triple Extension, you'll need to picture a push-off leg in which the ankle, knee, and hip joints are completely locked out.

Why Triple Extension is Vital

For this section, you'll need to refer to a video on YouTube. Type "Christian Coleman 40 Yard Dash" and click the 49-second video of Christian Coleman running a world record 4.12 second 40 yard dash. He runs the 40 faster than anybody at the NFL combine has ever run. *Sports Vidz. (2017, May 2). "CHRISTIAN COLEMAN FASTEST 40 YARD DASH EVER!" Interestingly, he does so by utilizing the very sprinting techniques you're learning in this book.

At the 23 second mark of the video, there is a brief slow-motion frame where you can clearly see him completely extending his leg as he drives out of the 3-point stance (it's very brief, so stay focused while watching). Rewind this slo-mo frame and watch it again and again, burning the image into your mind while visualizing yourself using the same sprint start technique. Take note that you cannot see the Triple Extension in the real-time version of the race, as it happens so quickly.

When Triple Extension is properly executed, the sprint start becomes a series of *bounds* even more so than a "running" motion. So, what are the mechanical principles underlying Triple Extension which make it give you a more explosive sprint start? The name of the game is *efficiency*.

Most athletes think the name of the game is *quickness*, but efficient strides beat quick strides. Check out any Olympic sprinter in slow-motion, and you'll see them triple extending. Yet, this technique somehow passes by most high school and collegiate football players and coaches. Give yourself an edge at the combine and on the playing field by adopting this OSRM.

Powerful, efficient strides will propel your body along the turf at higher speeds than more frequent, quick strides. I've found that most athletes do not triple extend for this very reason: In their minds, they don't feel "quick." It takes an extra split second to triple extend, and they want to get their foot down quickly to begin the next step. While getting the foot down quickly gives an athlete the *illusion* of being fast, the reality of the matter is that the athlete would run faster over 40 yards if Triple Extension was performed. It's not about how quickly your limbs are moving, it's about how fast your entire body moves over the ground. Do not fall into the trap of sacrificing powerful strides for quick, choppy movements.

Again, the 40 yard dash is not about quickness; it's about efficiency. Two specific variables determine efficiency: 1) **Power** and 2) **Technique**. The more powerful you are, the further you will propel your body toward the finish line with each step. All else being equal, more powerful leg muscles might propel the body 3" further with each individual stride than less powerful leg muscles. Over the course of an entire 40 yard dash, 3" per stride adds up. Next time you run a practice 40, count your strides, then multiply your number of strides times 3" ('3"' denotes 3-inches). **# Strides x 3-Inches = X-Inches** (read "number of strides times 3-inches equals this many inches"). You'll see there is a lot to be gained from more powerful push off. Even over just 10 strides, you're pulling ahead by 30", which is 2.5 feet. 2.5 feet is the difference between getting tackled and creating enough space between yourself and a defender to evade the tackle. It's the difference between the other team barely slipping into the end zone and preventing a touchdown from being scored, forcing your opponent to kick a field goal.

Now, the other variable that determines efficiency: Technique. The better your technique is, the less wasted movement you will have. Less wasted movement is a very good thing. It results in reaching the finish line in less time.

To reiterate this point, athletes, you need to shift your mindset. Instead of going for quick strides that "seem" fast, go for efficient strides. Let your leg triple extend off the starting line, just like the world's current fastest man in the 40 yard dash does (watch the video again to refresh your mind). Remember, this technique will not feel "quick," and that's okay because it creates more forward propulsion power. To be clear, you're not purposely moving slowly. Instead, you're moving as powerfully, and yes, even as quickly, as possible without sacrificing range of motion in the process. So, the goal is still to move quickly but with the execution of definitive Triple Extension. Do not cut your range of motion short in the name of faster steps. *Again*, you're moving as quickly as you can without sacrificing Triple Extension. By triple extending instead of cutting your step short, you cover distance more efficiently and, therefore, in less time.

When you do successfully triple extend, you'll notice a difference when taking off from the line. There will be more of a "pop," like you're shooting or springing off the line, as opposed to an ordinary step. It will feel more like a vertical jump (but performed horizontally and off of one leg) than running.

Over Striding

With all this talk about being patient and triple extending, a word needs to be said about overstriding. Triple extending and achieving efficient strides is not synonymous with overstriding. When I say your strides will be longer as a result of Triple Extension, it's because the push-off leg is propelling your body further down the turf. This is a major distinction from overstriding. Overstriding means you are reaching your leg in front of your body. In other words, attempting to gain distance by reaching with the lead leg, as opposed to gaining distance by more powerfully and efficiently driving through the push-off leg. See the difference? Both Triple Extension and overstriding will lead to longer strides; however, one does so by improving push off while the other does so by reaching with the lead leg.

The problem with reaching is it increases ground contact times. You absolutely cannot drive off the ground again until the foot on the ground reaches a center of gravity point beneath the body. Attempting to do so would result in a face plant, or at the very least, a stumble. A proper push off the ground takes place when the push-off foot is at the center of gravity point beneath the body. "Reaching" in order to increase stride length drastically increases the amount of time it takes to hit the center of gravity point and, therefore, the amount of time your foot will stay on the ground. Upon touching down to the ground, the reaching leg is way out in front of the center of gravity point. The body then pulls itself forward until the foot is directly beneath the body, at which time it can then initiate pushing off the ground. This "reaching" technique slows momentum, increases ground contact times, and as a result, makes your 40 time much slower. Triple Extension, on the other hand, allows longer forward propulsion distances with each stride without increasing ground contact times. Can you see how longer strides and shorter ground contact times will make you run faster, as opposed to longer strides and longer ground contact times? To improve your 40 time, longer strides must have nothing to do with reaching forward, and everything to do with how efficiently you push off the ground. When triple extending, you will forcefully plant the lead foot directly on the center of gravity point when making ground contact, making the foot immediately ready to drive off the ground. This concept leads us to the next OSRM.

Drive Phase OSRM #2

Up-and-Forward to Down-and-Back

This singular Olympic Sprinter Running Mechanic will be split into two parts. We'll break down the details in a moment but, first, understand that Up-and-Forward to Down-and-Back takes place as one fluid motion of the cycling leg during sprinting (cycling leg is the leg off the ground). The Up-and-Forward movement leads smoothly into the Down-and-Back movement with each stride. With that in mind know that although I'm splitting the description into two parts, in practice you will blend the two parts together as one fluid Cyclical Leg Action.

Dragging the foot just barely over the turf or actually on the turf is another common mistake athletes make in the 40 yard dash sprint start. Since you already have the video pulled up, re-watch the slow-motion portion of Christian Coleman setting the 40 yard dash world record (23-second mark). This time, you're not looking for Triple Extension, rather, you're looking at his cycling foot (foot in the air) just before it touches back down to the ground. Notice the point when the foot is above the ground and lingers there for just a split second. Then, it powerfully punches downward into the ground.

From the moment his foot leaves the ground, it moves in an Up-and-Forward direction. This Up-and-Forward movement is much different than dragging the foot just barely above the turf. The difference can be found in the *airspace* between the bottom of the foot and the turf. Before driving the foot back into the ground for the next stride, there needs to be sufficient airspace between the bottom of your foot and turf. This airspace is vital.

Imagine you are going to punch a heavy bag. Will your fist apply more power into the bag if you hold it 3" away from the bag and then punch, or if you stand an arm's length away and then apply your fist into the bag? Unless you're Bruce Lee, the answer is obviously the second option -- an arm's length away.

Standing farther from the bag gives your body a larger range of motion to create power before making contact with the bag. In the same way, your leg will be able to apply more power into the turf if there is more airspace between the bottom of your foot and the ground. If you drag your foot too close to the ground, there is not enough space between the bottom of your foot and the turf, and your leg will not be able to produce nearly as much power as it drives Down-and-Back into the ground.

An Up-and-Forward action is so important because it creates space between the bottom of your foot and the ground. As described a moment ago, this airspace is vital because it allows the foot to more powerfully apply force Down-and-Back into the ground. Don't just passively let your foot fall to the ground. *Drive* that sucker into the turf with force.

I understand not every visualization resonates with every individual athlete, so if the punching bag visualization didn't lead to a stronger understanding of this concept, this next one will. Picture yourself holding a basketball. Is it going to bounce higher if you passively drop it to the ground, or if you forcefully throw it into the ground? Like the heavy bag example, the answer is obvious. In the same way, you will more powerfully propel your body forward during the 40 yard dash sprint start by forcefully driving your foot Down-and-Back into the ground with each stride.

To be clear, this is not at all like the chicken and egg conundrum. Which came first, the chicken or the egg? Who knows. Eggs make chickens, and chickens make eggs. But, if the question is *which came first, the Up-and-Forward action, or the*

Down-and-Back action?, the answer is clear. Up-and-Forward. Without Up-and-Forward, Down-and-Back absolutely cannot happen. And without Down-and-Back, explosive forward propulsion absolutely cannot happen.

Up-and-Forward → Down-and-Back → Explosive Forward Propulsion → Faster 40 Time

From the starting line, and with each subsequent step of the Drive Phase, the rear foot moves Up-and-Forward. This Up-and-Forward action creates airspace between the bottom of the foot and the turf. The airspace gives your foot the room it needs to forcefully deliver power into the turf. This forceful delivery of power in turn propels the body forward in an explosive manner, which is the entire point, as explosive forward propulsion results in faster times.

Another important detail here is a foot position called dorsiflexion. If you're unfamiliar with the term, plantarflexion is when the toes are pointed down, as displayed by ballerinas and gymnasts. On the other hand, *dorsiflexion* refers to pulling the toes up toward the knee, as displayed by Olympic sprinters. Notice that Christian Coleman's toes are dorsiflexed, pulled up toward the knee, just before driving his foot back down into the turf. You'll need to view the slo-mo portion of the video to see this clearly, which you can find at the 23-second mark. His toes are obviously and definitively pulled up toward his knee like the elite sprinter he is, and not pointed downward toward the turf like a ballerina.

Dorsiflexion can come off as a minor detail, especially because the difference between proper dorsiflexion and a lack thereof is a matter of just a couple inches. There are two primary reasons why dorsiflexion is so important:

1) It prevents you from stumbling over the turf. Often, an athlete attempting to run the 40 yard dash will drive off the line, only to stumble within the first few strides because his toes were pointed down and caught the turf. Not good.

2) The second reason why dorsiflexion is important is that it sets you up in a powerful position which allows you to immediately begin driving off the ground once you touch the turf. In other words, dorsiflexion reduces ground contact times. Speed, largely, is about minimizing ground contact times, and dorsiflexion does exactly that. The aim of any athlete who wants to sprint fast is to drive off the ground as powerfully as possible but spend minimal time on the ground.

If you touch the turf with your toes pointed downward like a ballerina, you're going to spend *more* time on the ground because now your ankle needs to flex to bring more of the foot into contact with the ground before driving off again. Yes, a decent portion of the foot is in contact with the ground before driving off, specifically, about 2/3. Having 2/3 of the foot touching the turf allows you to drive through the balls of your feet, the most stable, powerful part of the foot. Much stronger than the toes.

Back to ground-contact time: When an athlete touches the ground in a dorsiflexed position (toes up), the foot is prepared to drive off the ground as soon as it makes contact. There is no need to first flex the ankle, bringing more of the foot to the ground, then driving off into the next stride. It's ready to go.

Drive Phase OSRM #3
Elongated Torso

Since the angle of the Christian Coleman 40 yard dash video is not sufficient to exemplify this third key, I am going to refer you to another video. On YouTube, watch "Asafa Powell Start" by Daniel Ryan. *Daniel Ryan. (2016, February 20). "Asafa Powell Start". Be sure you don't accidentally watch the video by Denis Eridiri, as this was performed for advertising purposes, and is not a sprint start that would be used in a competitive situation. If you're not familiar with Powell, he is a Jamaican sprinter who held the 100m world record before Usain Bolt entered the scene.

In this video, it will be easy to notice Powell's Triple Extension, as well as his Up-and-Forward to Down-and-Back leg movement as he drives off the line. Next, and this is OSRM #3 of the Drive Phase, notice his Elongated Torso. In other words, his torso is not hunched downward, like an arch. It is elongated, flat like a board, and sturdy.

What is the benefit of an Elongated Torso as opposed to a hunched back? Simply stated, power transfer. Go back to the punching bag example from earlier. This time you have two weapon choices: a swimming noodle or a blunt staff made of strong, sturdy material. If your goal is to hit the bag and have no effect whatsoever, you would choose to hit it with the swimming noodle. However, if your goal is to transfer as much of your muscular force into the bag as possible, the blunt spear will be your better bet. Obvious choice. The key question linking this concept to running a faster 40 yard dash is, *"What exactly is it about the staff that makes it capable of transferring more force into the bag than the swimming noodle?"*

The answer is that the material of the staff is sturdy. With both the noodle and the staff, your *muscles* are creating the same amount of muscular force. It has little to do with the origin of the force, which is the energy created by your muscles, and everything to do with the ability of the object you are using as a weapon to *transfer* force from your muscles into the destination point of the bag. The sturdy staff transfers force differently than the wobbly noodle. A noodle can't transfer force because of its *unstable* nature. Instability dissipates force. In the same way, a forward rolling back cannot transfer force. Instead, due to the weak, unstable nature of a hunched back, it dissipates force, creating the negative result of less forward propulsion.

Consider this: Your legs can be creating an insanely high amount of power; but if your torso is weak and hunched forward, that high amount of power will dissipate, and it won't be used to propel you down the turf with speed. By maintaining an elongated, strong, sturdy torso, the power you create is *transferred* into the turf which then propels your body forward.

Drive Phase OSRM #4
Powerful Arm Action

Powerful Arm Action will keep your body in balance during the sprint start. If your arms are not *offsetting* your legs, then you're going to run in a zigzag fashion. That is, when you drive off the ground with your right leg, your body is going to propel itself not only forward but also slightly to the left. Then, when you drive off the ground with your left leg, your body is going to propel itself slightly to the right. Zig. Zag. In order to drive your body *forward* and minimize left-right movements, you must use Powerful Arm Action.

Drive those arms like your life depends on it. Depending upon your body structure, it may not suit you to keep your arms moving in a perfectly straight front-to-back motion. In general, leaner athletes can maintain front to back arm action that moves in more of a straight line. That is, their elbows don't bow outside as much during the backswing portion of the movement. On the other hand, athletes with well-developed, wide latissimus dorsi muscles (the thick muscles of the back) may be better off with a slight outward angle to their arm action. Take note of the word *slight*. Do not swing your arms from side-to-side. We're still talking about a forward to backward motion. The reason a slight angle is acceptable for the athlete with a wider back is that it would require more muscular tension to hold the elbows close to the body than allowing them to swing in a natural motion.

Again, Powerful Arm Action offsets leg action, allowing you to run in a *straight line* with each stride as opposed to zigzagging your way down the turf. When setting your rear arm for the 40 yard dash 3-point stance sprint start, allow the angle of the rear arm's elbow joint to widen. To feel this out, try this: Stand up and bend forward slightly at the waist without letting your back hunch forward with your left foot up front and the right foot in back. Bend your knees a bit if you want. Your torso should be at a 45° angle to the ground and straight like a board. Now, bring your right arm forward and your left arm back. Notice where your left arm, the arm moving to the back of the body, naturally wants to stop. After you've noticed where that point is, pull it another 1-2" farther back, and that is where you want to be when performing your 3-point 40 yard dash start. This position sets the arm in such a way that it is ready to *shoot* forward, like releasing a loaded spring or stretching a rubber band back and letting it go.

Your arm action technique will be similar to this as you are actually striding along the turf.

Arm action will be more exaggerated earlier in the event and less exaggerated as your transition out of your Drive Phase and into your Upright Running Phase. As your body naturally moves from an angle that is closer to the ground during the Drive Phase to a completely vertical position in the Upright Running Phase, your arm action will naturally follow suit. If you follow the OSRMs laid out in this book, you won't need to concern yourself with forcing your body angles in relationship to the turf, as the angles will naturally take care of themselves so long as you are maintaining an Elongated Torso, triple extending, using Up-and-Forward to Down-and-Back leg action, and forcefully pumping your arms.

To elaborate on the movement of the arms, at the start of the 40, your elbow joint will widen as it moves to the back of the body, and close as it moves to the front of the body. The widening at the back of the body creates a rubber band-like effect in the shoulder and chest muscles, which then slings the arm to the front of the body in a powerful manner. The widening of the elbow joint also takes longer to complete than a bent elbow range of motion. This is important because it provides the extra split second needed to triple extend, as opposed to using short, choppy strides. Bending the elbow at the front of the body, on the other hand, creates a braking effect, which counteracts the opposite leg (the leg in the air), preventing it from over striding and encouraging it to drive Down-and-Back into the turf.

How Far Should I Place My Front Foot from the Line?

Someone will inevitably ask, "How far from the line should my front foot be?" Most people are looking for an exact number such as five inches. It doesn't work that way. Body type and strength are two factors that play an enormous role in determining how far back your foot needs to be from the line. You want to be at a place where there is enough space to successfully put your body into the positions we are going to discuss in this 3-Point Stance Phase section.

If your body is too scrunched then you will not be able to put your body in the positions we discuss here, and your ability to explode off the line will suffer. On the other hand, you don't want to be too far back from the line either. What you *do* want is a middle ground position. In other words, your front leg is definitely feeling the pressure, but not so much so that your ability to explode off the line is lessened. If you're feeling especially scrunched up on the starting line, moving just an inch back will do wonders in the area of improving your ability to explode off the line with high velocity.

Consider the mechanics of moving back just a tad: If you're on the leg press, will you be able to push more weight if you begin from a position where the seat is all the way forward, resulting in tightly scrunched legs *or*, from a position where the seat is further back resulting in more open (wider) knee and hip angles? From the scrunched position, it's harder to get started. The same applies to your 40 yard dash start. I know you want to be as close to the line as possible, but sometimes the extra pressure on your front leg isn't worth the single inch you gain from moving closer. To review, settle yourself into a position where your front leg is definitely feeling "loaded," but not so loaded that your ability to explode off the line is compromised.

Take Your Time

This next concept will seem counterintuitive, and it's one of the most challenging concepts to teach novice athletes. "Novice" refers to your training age, not your best time. Just because you're already sprinting faster than most athletes your age doesn't mean you've come close to reaching your maximum potential. The novice lineman running a 4.9 40 can be the same training age as the novice running back running a 4.5 40. Having natural speed does not remove you from the novice category. What removes you from the novice category is a period of time, at least two years, dedicated to improving your skill, thereby maximizing your personal window of potential.

More experienced athletes are more apt to immediately grasping this "take your time" concept. The experienced athlete sees beneath the surface, whereas the novice athlete may have difficulty separating the forest from the trees. That is, the novice athlete sees the big picture: "Wow, that Olympic sprinter just broke a world record! He's so fast." On the other hand, the experienced athlete can notice the forest, but also see each individual tree: "Awesome world record sprint. I wonder which technical variables played a role in his ability to run such a fast time?"

In discussing this "take your time" concept, you must put on the mindset of an experienced athlete. If you don't, it will make no sense to you, and you'll end up discarding one of the most important factors involved in improving your 40 yard dash time.

Go back to the "Asafa Powell Start" video by Daniel Ryan. The way he sprints is distinctly different from the way most football players sprint. Powell takes his time to completely extend his limbs. If you watch closely, you'll notice that he even "floats" over the ground (while still moving forward) for a brief moment with each stride. When running a 40 yard dash, most football players go for quick steps. What ends up happening is that their sprint start rhythm becomes short and choppy, as opposed to efficient and powerful.

You can see the same technique in the Christian Coleman 40 yard dash. Unfortunately, his entire 40 is not in slow-motion. This technical concept is hardly noticeable to even the most well-trained eye at full speed execution, so noticing an athlete perform this will be challenging if the video is not in slo-mo. At the 23 second mark in the video, you can clearly see this "take your time" concept in action, as the video briefly plays in slow-motion. He takes his time extending his legs and briefly floats over the turf before powerfully driving the other foot back into the ground.

This is huge! Short, choppy steps "feel" faster. Don't be fooled by this. It is an illusion. The reason short, choppy steps feel faster is because your arms and legs are taking more steps per 10 yards covered. You're taking more frequent steps, but this doesn't necessarily mean you are covering distance at a faster speed. Efficient, powerful steps are what will move you along the turf at the fastest possible speed, but these steps will not feel as fast to the athlete performing them. Again, go back and check out the Asafa Powell and Christian Coleman slo-mo videos. Their steps are powerful and efficient when viewed in slow-motion. If you viewed them sprinting at full speed, you couldn't tell the difference, so don't let your eyes deceive you. That's why a resource such as this is vital to your development as an athlete: It opens your eyes to performance-enhancing factors previously unnoticeable to you. In order to best view your own or another athlete's 40 yard dash Drive Phase technique, use the slow-motion recording option on your smartphone. I've been training athletes in the sprint start for 12 years at the time of this writing, and my eyes still miss things at full-speed execution that I easily notice when watching a slow-motion playback.

The take-your-time mindset will feel awkward to you the first time you attempt it. Stick with it, because this concept alone will give you a major edge over other athletes. For example, check out Barry Sanders, the best running back to ever play the game (in my humble opinion). Most people admire him for his insane jukes and crazy cuts. They can't sing his praises enough when it comes to those two areas. **However**, and this is huge, let me tell you why I admire Barry Sanders so much as a running back.

Yes, his "moves" are insane. But, if you watch his highlights, you'll notice what he does *after* his juke. He creates serious, enormous distance between himself and the defender. Which mindset does he use to create this distance? That's right -- it's the take-your-time mindset! He triple extends, taking his time to completely push off the ground. His steps, when accelerating away from the defender after the juke, are not even close to short and choppy. Like Asafa Powell and Christian Coleman, two of the best Olympic sprinters in history, he uses powerful, efficient strides.

Get short and choppy strides out of your mind right now. They will not result in your fastest possible 40 yard dash times. Remember, just because short and choppy feels faster for the reason of shorter ranges of motion of the arms and legs, this does not make your body move faster over 40 yards. Watch Powell and

Coleman in slo-mo over and over. Apply OSRM #1 and visualize yourself using their powerful, efficient stride technique. Engrain it into your mind.

Upright Running Phase

Transition

From the Drive Phase, you will transition to the Upright Running Phase. Avoid forcing yourself into the upright position and instead gradually allow your body to rise up as you sprint down the turf. There is never a specific point when you abruptly go from driving to upright running. It's a gradual lifting process. Due to the gradual nature of the process, a well-executed transition from the Drive Phase to the Upright Running Phase will hardly be noticeable, may even be unconscious, to the athlete executing it.

Watch various athletes run the 40, and what you'll often see is an athlete drive out and stay low followed by suddenly popping up into a vertical running position 4-6 steps into the sprint. The most important reason why this is detrimental is because your body uses different muscle fibers during the Drive Phase than during the Upright Running Phase portion of the race. If you pop up just five strides into the race, you're going to tax the specific muscle fibers involved in the upright portion of the race for the remainder of the 40 yard dash.

On the other hand, if you split your 40 into approximate thirds, 1/3 drive phase, 1/3 transition, and 1/3 Upright Running Phase, the energy systems of your muscle fibers won't be struggling to hang on. In other words, by extending your Drive Phase, you've used different muscle fibers for the acceleration portion of the 40, and now you have fresh muscle cells available for the upright running, top speed maintenance portion of the race.

Make no bones about it- unless you are a genetic freak like Usain Bolt, popping up at the beginning of the 40 yard dash will fatigue the muscles you are meant to use in the second half of the event, and you will struggle to complete the last 15 yards of the race in a smooth, powerful fashion. With that in mind, go back and watch the Christian Coleman and Asafa Powell videos on YouTube, and practice the correlating OSRM first by visualizing in your mind and then physically executing.

You've transitioned from the Drive Phase to the Upright Running Phase, so it's time to examine the key components of the upright running portion of the 40 yard dash.

There are three concepts to keep in mind about the Upright Running Phase. They are:

1. Loose Shoulders
2. Elevated Torso
3. Cyclical Leg Action

Upright Running Phase OSRM #1
Loose Shoulders

Loose Shoulders. Pull that Christian Coleman 40 yard dash video up again. In the last five seconds of the video, you get a slow-motion peak at his Upright Running Phase of the race. Take a look at his shoulders and face. His shoulders aren't lifted up toward his neck, causing strain and tension. His face is loose and relaxed, not grimacing in an attempt to "try harder." Most uninformed athletes tighten their shoulders in a misguided attempt to "dig deep" and therefore run faster. Unfortunately, this method does not have the desired effect. The only effect tightening the shoulders and face has is that of slower times.

Tight shoulders mean more effort to move the shoulder joint. More effort to move the shoulder joint means more tension in the body. More tension in the body means . . . you guessed it: Slower moving limbs. And what do slower moving limbs mean? Slower sprinting speeds.

When running the 40 yard dash, you want your limbs to move as freely and fluidly as possible. The more free they are to move through a repeated back-and-forth range of motion, the more power your limbs will consistently produce over the course of an entire 40 yard sprint. The more power your limbs produce, the faster your body will propel itself forward.

Think of sprinting as a series of individual forward propulsions, as opposed to one big 40 yard run. First, the left leg propels your body forward, then the right leg. Over and over. Fast times are the result of maximizing *each individual* propulsion. By sprinting with free-flowing, fluidly moving limbs, each individual forward propulsion is maximized.

Let me exemplify this point about Loose Shoulders. As a sophomore collegiate track and field athlete, I was in a close 100m dash race with a teammate. We were neck and neck with 15 meters to go in the race. For a brief moment, I started trying harder. "Digging deep." I quickly noticed I wasn't gaining the lead through these efforts. My arms and legs were *already* driving and pumping with as much power as they could muster. It wasn't a matter of trying *harder*; it was a matter of *minimizing muscle tension* as much as possible so my arms and legs could move in a free-flowing manner. Minimizing muscle tension. I noticed that trying harder created more tension in my neck and shoulder areas. I simply let my shoulders drop and hang loose while still pumping with the same intensity. Immediately, I gained the lead by just enough to edge out my teammate at the finish line.

For most athletes, they interpret staying loose as "low effort" or not giving their best. This is not even close to the truth. The key is to keep your shoulders relaxed without relinquishing effort or intensity. Let me put it this way: The muscles in your face are not going to aid, in any manner whatsoever, with propelling your body more explosively over 40 yards, so don't tighten them! Keep your face relaxed. Similarly, while a forward and backward motion of the shoulder joint is key in propelling yourself over 40 yards, there is no reason for the shoulders to vertically lift up toward your ears. By keeping your shoulders loose and low (as opposed to tight and high), you will significantly decrease muscle tension, which means your free-moving limbs will be able to more explosively propel your body forward.

There will always be muscle tension in your body during the 40 yard dash because by its very nature, the race requires your muscles to contract. The term "stay loose" means learning to engage only the muscles required to sprint. As described a moment ago, if a muscle isn't required to sprint, don't flex that muscle. This especially includes the muscles of the face and the muscles on top of the shoulders, popularly known as *the traps*, short for "trapezius." Keep loose, reduce muscle tension, and watch your times improve as a result of creating fluid, free-flowing limb movement.

Upright Running Phase OSRM #2
Elevated Torso

This is similar to an Elongated Torso, as described in the Drive Phase section, but the body angle is different. During the Drive Phase, the body is closer to a horizontal angle in relationship to the ground. During the Upright Running Phase, on the other hand, the body is completely vertical in relationship to the ground.

As you now know, the tendency during the Drive Phase for most athletes is to roll the spine forward, creating a hunch in the back. In contrast, the tendency during the Upright Running Phase is to arch the torso backward. Conversely, athletes who display a slight forward lean during the Upright Running Phase typically do so due to the genetic shape of their spine. "Lordosis" is the term that describes a lower back that excessively curves inward. If you can picture it, the spine curves toward the belly button in an exaggerated manner. The excessive inward curve causes the athlete's glutes, or buttocks, to protrude backward. So, imagine a lower back that is pushed in, causing the belly to protrude slightly forward and the buttocks to protrude slightly backward.

If you have the spinal genetics described above, Lordosis, you may naturally lean *slightly* forward during the Upright Running Phase, while still maintaining as upright a position as possible. If this does not describe your genetic makeup, you will be completely vertical during the Upright Running Phase.

Back to the Elevated Torso. The purpose of maintaining an Elevated Torso is that it holds your hips high. High hip posture, as opposed to dropped, low hips, allows the legs more spaciousness to *freely* rotate beneath your body. The more space there is between the bottom of the hips and the ground, the more freely your legs can rotate, and therefore the more powerfully they can propel your body forward. Once again, this is the concept of free-flowing limb movement, as described in the section about Loose Shoulders.

You can tell when sprinters are tired during practice because their hips will drop. Counterintuitively, high hip posture is not as much about hip strength as it is about core strength. The importance of the core in developing fast sprinting speed simply cannot be highlighted enough. It is absolutely central in maintaining the body postures which result in maximal limb power output. If the core cannot maintain its posture and gives out due to lack of development, your times . . . will . . . get . . . slower. If you collapse backward during the Upright Running Phase, that is, your back arches backward, it is a sure sign that your core is underdeveloped. The same applies to your ability to maintain an Elongated Torso during the Drive Phase portion of the 40 yard dash.

[Begin rant] Most athletes and coaches do not understand just how much is asked of the core during the 40 yard dash. As a matter of fact, most don't realize how much is asked of the core during sports, period. I've heard of football strength and conditioning programs involving no core work. #LOL. In terms of athletic performance, biceps are absolutely, positively, not more important than the core! If you have to choose between one or the other, choose core. [End rant]

Specifically, in what way is the core being called upon during the 40 yard dash? When sprinting, serious levels of force are produced. The core must be able to *absorb* the impact of that force without bending, as a tree blowing in the wind would bend. If the core does not absorb the majority of the impact force during sprinting, then it's solely up to the legs, resulting in longer ground contact times due to an increased need for leg stabilization with each stride. Unlike the right and left legs, which take turns absorbing impact forces with each stride down the turf, the core must absorb impact forces on *every step*, with no break, during the entire 40 yards. That is a lot to ask, and it can only be done successfully with a well-developed core.

The lower part of the abdomen is the primary workhorse when it comes to maintaining an Elevated Torso. When people think of the "ab muscles," they typically think of the 6-pack area of the abdomen. Much more important than the 6-pack area is the part of the abdomen that is below the 6-pack. These are truly your "lower abs," a term normally assigned to the bottom two muscles that make up the 6-pack. When this lower portion of the core is not well-developed, the torso will give way like a tree bending in the wind, resulting in low-hip posture. Low-hip posture then negatively affects the ability of your legs to freely and fluidly cycle below the torso. In order to maximize your sprinting speed, your legs must be able to cycle freely and fluidly.

Part of the cure for a lack of an Elevated Torso is simply being aware of it. Most athletes aren't aware of the vital role the core plays in sprinting speed and can correct their posture after becoming aware. However, if your core is underdeveloped, simply being aware of it won't be enough. You will need to perform core strengthening exercises as well as practice running with an Elevated Torso. Both of these will aid in strengthening your core in a way that maximizes sprinting speed.

Although strength training is not within the scope of this book, here's an important tip in the area of core development: Keep your hip flexors loose. On days when you do core work, thoroughly stretch the hip flexors immediately afterward and again just before going to bed. Stretch them on non-core days as well.

Many core exercises involve the hip flexors. If they become too tight, a litany of problems can arise, from lower back to hamstring, and even knee issues. I have my athletes do *some* abdominal exercises that involve the hip flexors. However, if an athlete has a case of Lordosis, pain in the lower back, or tightness in the hamstrings, I completely avoid any core exercises that involve the hip flexors. Given the preexisting physical conditions in addition to the fact that there are plenty of abdominal exercises that do not involve the hip flexors, it's simply not worth the risk.

On the other hand, for athletes without these preexisting conditions, they can safely perform ab exercises that involve the hip flexors (leg lifts, reverse crunches, bicycles, etc.). However, there a*bsolutely* must be a balance between core exercises that do involve the hip flexors and exercises that do not, or you risk taking an athlete from having no back issues to developing a new issue. Use 70/30 as a guide: 70% without hip flexor involvement and 30% with hip flexor involvement. As a starting point, Google or YouTube "McGill 3" and apply those exercises. Then, stretch thoroughly to offset tightness.

Upright Running Phase OSRM #3

Cyclical Leg Action

In order to produce forward propulsion in the most explosive manner, your leg action needs to be cyclical. Two common mistakes when it comes to leg action in the Upright Running Phase are a) low-swinging leg action and b) vertical leg action.

Low-swinging leg action creates an oval-shaped path of motion as opposed to circular. The foot lifts off the ground slightly, but there is minimal knee lift and, therefore, minimal power production Down-and-Back into the ground. In the Drive Phase section, the importance of airspace between the bottom of the foot and the ground for the purpose of producing max force was discussed. As mentioned earlier, if you're going to punch a punching bag, will you develop more power holding your fist 2" from the bag or standing back 2', drawing your arm back, and then stepping into the bag? The second option will obviously produce more force. In the same way, when your foot is close to the ground, as is the case during low-swinging leg action, there is no room for your leg to produce force back down into the ground. On the other hand, when there is adequate airspace between the bottom of the foot and the ground, there is time and space for the leg to create maximum force as the foot drives into the turf.

Vertical leg action, on the other hand, happens when you run with high knee lift but little horizontal cycling action. As a reminder, *low-swinging leg action* takes place when you use long, horizontal strides with little vertical cyclical movement; *vertical leg action* takes place when there is high, vertical leg action but little horizontal cyclical action. Vertical leg action maximizes upward lift of the body but does not result in maximal *forward* propulsion. The action of sprinting consists of a *balance* between upward propulsion and horizontal propulsion of the body. Going to the extreme with one or the other will not allow the leg to create maximum force before the foot touches the ground.

With vertical leg action, there is beyond adequate airspace between the ground and the bottom of the foot. However, that airspace translates into undesirable vertical propulsion, not the desirable forward propulsion of the body and, therefore, doesn't result in faster times. In order to translate adequate airspace into explosive forward propulsion of the body down the turf, the leg must perform a Down-and-Back action, not only down (as takes place in vertical leg action), which brings us to **OSRM #3 of the Upright Running Phase**: *Cyclical Leg Action*.

With Cyclical Leg Action, you strike a balance between low swinging leg action and vertical leg action, thus maximizing sprinting speed. The concept in the following sentence will be described in more detail in a moment, but here is a brief introduction to the concept: The "back" action in the Down-and-Back leg cycle is what ensures forward propulsion of the body. Remember learning Newton's Law in school? It goes like this: **For every action, there is an equal and opposite reaction.** So, think about Newton's Law in terms of sprinting and the way your legs move while sprinting. If your leg action is only **down**, the *opposite* reaction will be **up**. As described a moment ago, this is not what you want.

Now, the details of Cyclical Leg Action. During the Upright Running Phase, there will be a brief point in time when one of your legs is still in contact with the ground, but the joints of that leg are fully locked. That is, the leg is completely extended (Triple Extension) and *about* to leave the ground but has not yet left the ground. This will be our starting point for describing Cyclical Leg Action. From the starting point of the leg being completely extended and about to leave the ground, the process looks like this:

     a) Heel to butt

     b) Pull through the hips

     c) Down-and-Back into the ground

Heel to Butt

The heel goes directly to the buttocks, pulls through the hip area, and then moves in a Down-and-Back fashion toward the ground. The foot then pushes off the ground and repeats the cycle. Now, when I say the heel goes directly to the buttocks, I don't mean you actually have to physically touch your heel to your butt. The point here is the heel moving directly from the ground toward the butt instead of swooping upward above the buttocks. More lean, flexible players may actually have the heel physically touch the butt, whereas more muscular players will simply move the heel in a straight line directly toward the buttocks without the two ever actually touching.

As alluded to, a common mistake athletes make at this point is bringing the heel up *behind* the buttocks and then forward and through the hips. By bringing the heel directly *to* the buttocks, no movement is wasted, and each stride is made as efficiently as possible. Further, there is less tension on the hamstrings (swooping upward causes more hamstring tension). On the other hand, when the heel rises up behind the hips and is then drawn to the front of the body, unnecessary pressure is placed on the hamstring muscle, and the cyclical motion takes longer to complete. Over the course of an entire 40 yards, this lack of efficiency will make a difference in a negative way.

To be clear, this is not to say that the foot is never behind the body. It has to temporarily find itself behind the body because the torso continues moving forward as the push-off leg stays on the ground. At the point when the push-off leg is completely locked, the foot is behind the body as the torso is propelled forward. The key to Cyclical Leg Action is to bring the heel directly to the bottom of the buttocks after pushing off the ground and not waste motion by lifting the heel up and behind the body. Imagine the heel reaching the buttocks in a straight line, as opposed to a swooping manner.

Through the Hips

This is the most simple, effortless portion of Cyclical Leg Action. Once the heel reaches the buttocks, the knee lifts slightly, naturally pulling the heel forward. Once pulled forward, the heel is in front of the body.

To review: Bring the heel directly to the buttocks with minimal upward lift behind the body. Next, let the heel be naturally pulled to a position in front of the body.

Down-and-Back

This is where forward propulsion power is created. Now that your heel is in front of the body, let it move to a position directly below the knee. This *doesn't* mean your toes are directly below the knee. It means your *heel* is directly below the knee. By default, this means your toes will be slightly in front of the knee. Being in a position where your heel is directly below the knee sets your leg up for a powerful Down-and-Back action. On the other hand, if your toes are below the knee, your Down-and-Back action will be compromised and not produce as much power.

Think back to Newton's Law. By having your toes slightly in front of your knee and your heel directly below the knee, there is more horizontal distance between the heel of your front leg and the knee of the rear leg. If you bring your toes back and under your knee, your heel then moves into a position below the thigh instead of below the knee, which brings it closer to the knee of the rear leg. By creating *more* horizontal distance between the heel of the lead leg and the knee of the rear leg, there is more room for the "back" portion in the Down-and-Back movement. Before moving on, go ahead and try this concept out. Stand on one leg with the knee of the other leg lifted into the air. Place your toes directly below your knee, then move the Ball of the Foot to the ground, touching down directly beneath you at your center of gravity point. Next, repeat the process, except this time your *heel* will be directly below the knee, which means your toes will be slightly in front of the knee. Notice how there is more space between the center of gravity point and the ball of your foot. More room to create power as the Ball of the Foot punches itself into the ground with each stride.

Now, this is important, so be sure to get this next part: Without this space, the Down-and-Back movement primarily becomes a down movement. Earlier, the inefficiency of a down movement without an accompanying "back" action was discussed. To review this concept, what's the equal and opposite reaction of a downward movement? An upward movement. The body must be propelled *up and forward*, not just up, if you want faster times. To create an equal and opposite reaction that maximizes sprinting speed, your leg action must move Down-and-Back (aka cyclically), of which the equal and opposite reaction is Up-and-Forward.

Let's review Cyclical Leg Action. Bring the heel directly to the buttocks in a movement that creates a straight line. Do not swoop the heel up behind the body. Next, let the heel naturally pull itself forward, as the knee raises, to a position in front of the body. Now, let the heel reach a position directly below the knee, then powerfully attack the ground with a Down-and-Back movement pattern. Land on the Ball of the Foot (not the toes), drive through the ground, and repeat.

Summary

3-Point Stance Phase

1. Hip Height
    a. Low hips don't provide enough space for the rear leg to drive forward without restriction. Keep the hips slightly higher than the shoulders.

2. Elongated torso
    a. An elongated torso ensures optimal power transfer and therefore maximizes forward propulsion of the body.

3. Ball of the Foot
    a. Stand on the Ball of the Foot. This engages the glutes, plus the Ball of the Foot is stronger and more stable than the toes.

Drive Phase

1. Triple Extension
    a. Although it may not feel "fast," it creates a powerful forward thrusting of the body.

2. Up-and-Forward to Down-and-Back

      b. Bringing the foot Up-and-Forward creates airspace between the bottom of the foot and the ground, which then gives the leg more time and space to develop power on the way down back to the ground.

3. Elongated Torso

      c. A sturdy torso maximizes the transfer of power. A weak torso dissipates power, making that power useless for forward propulsion of the body.

4. Powerful Arm Action

      d. Stabilizes the body and aids in propelling you forward.

Upright Running Phase

1. Loose Shoulders

      a. Releases muscular tension, freeing the arms to fluidly and powerfully complete a full range of motion.

2. Elevated Torso

      b. Keeps the hips high, which provides spaciousness for the legs to powerfully rotate beneath the body.

3. Cyclical Leg Action

      c. Bringing the heel directly to the glute, pulling it through, and then bringing it to a position directly below the knee creates maximum force back down into the ground, explosively propelling your body forward with each stride.

Putting It All Together

1. Get into a 3-Point stance with a sturdy torso, hips slightly elevated above shoulder height, and ball of the lead foot firmly placed on the ground.

2. As you drive out, vigorously pump your arms while triple extending on each stride, as well as bringing your other leg up-and-over and then Down-and-Back into the ground with great power.

3. Let your body gradually come to an upright running position. This should not happen suddenly. Once in an upright position, keep your torso elevated, stride your legs in a cyclical action, and stay relaxed in the shoulders and face without decreasing intensity.

Part III

Mindset

Improvement Mindset

Your mindset will determine whether you are successful in achieving faster speeds in the 40 yard dash. Actually, your mindset will determine the entire trajectory of your athletic career as well as your entire life.

Some athletes are naturally gifted but never develop beyond their genetic capabilities. When they lose, they throw big-boy or big-girl tantrums rather than asking how they can do better the next time. With this poor mindset, they will never fulfill their potential. There are professional athletes with this mindset. They throw things and punch people. They might reach the pinnacle of success in their sport, but they don't stay there for long because the competition for the top dog spot is crazy-heavy. Everybody is coming for them. The people who are coming for them are working to get better on a daily basis. Athletes with a poor mindset, however, think they should be able to achieve pinnacle performance and maintain that performance over a prolonged period without consistent improvement.

You must constantly ask how you can get better. *Constantly*. There's no resting at the top.

If you currently run a 4.6 40, ask how you can run a 4.5. When you run that 4.5, ask how you can run a 4.45. When you hit 4.45, ask how you can run 4.40. When you get there, ask how you can run a 4.35. "For everyone who asks receives, and the one who searches finds, and to the one who knocks, the door will be opened" (from Matthew 7:8). Constantly improve.

Okay, honesty time. I swiped the concept of an Improvement Mindset from the book "Mindset" by Carol Dweck, Ph.D. (*highly* recommended read). In her amazing book, Dweck discusses two mindsets. The first is the Fixed Mindset. What is the Fixed Mindset? It refers to the belief that if I need to work hard for something, I'm a failure. True success means I'm a natural and can get it right away, effortlessly. If I can't accomplish something immediately, I'm no good. Trying hard is for losers.

The second is the Growth Mindset. It refers to an attitude that says, "Where I'm at now is only the beginning. As I learn and practice, I'll constantly improve. With constant improvement, I can get to where I want to be."

With this mindset, there's no such thing as being dumb; there is only learning new study-methods in order to better learn new concepts. There is no such thing as being trapped playing JV for the duration of your high school athletic career. There is only daily improvement. Focus on the process. Ask the hard questions other athletes aren't asking. For example, "What, specifically, is it going to take for me to gain the skills, strength, and speed to be a major contributor at the varsity

[collegiate/professional] level?" Then, create specific actions based upon your answers. Do not just let the ideas float around in your head without taking action steps.

When you sit down and focus on a subject, your brain builds stronger neural pathways. This means that the subject becomes more and more second nature to you. Say you've never even heard of "The Hobbit" series by J.R.R. Tolkein. Could you write an 8-page paper about the symbolism found in these stories? No. Could you describe what the stories mean to you, personally? No. It's not because you're dumb, inadequate, or otherwise lacking. It's simply because you are *unfamiliar* with *The Hobbit* series.

Now, over the next six months, you read the books, watch the movies, and listen to the audiobooks. Simply by familiarizing yourself with the series, your neural pathways as they pertain to "The Hobbit" are 10x stronger than they were six months ago. You can easily go on about the symbolism of the series and how the various experiences the characters go through in the story relates to your own life.

Practicing your 40 yard dash sprinting technique *also* builds neural pathways. That's right. Your brain sends neurons down your spinal cord and into your muscle fibers. The stronger your neural pathways are, the more power your muscle fibers produce and, therefore, the faster you sprint. So, if you're of the mindset that you're "just slow and can't get any faster," think again. Actually, ditch that mindset immediately, and adopt the Growth Mindset, or as I prefer to call it regarding sports performance, the Improvement Mindset.

Everything in this book is designed to improve your neural pathways as they pertain to the physical action of sprinting. So if you're starting out with slower times than where you'd like to be, get excited, because you're about to get better, assuming you apply the techniques in this book.

Remember my personal story? I was in the middle of the pack in my conference as a freshman sprinter in college. Probably ranked something like 1000th in the nation. Not where I wanted to be. Not even close. So, I learned. I developed neural pathways. Without realizing it, I took on an Improvement Mindset. By senior year, I broke the conference meet record and placed 3rd in the nation.

If you want to improve, you can. However, it will take an Improvement Mindset on your part. An Improvement Mindset asks, "How can I overcome this obstacle?" It does not say, "This obstacle is going to hold me back." With a Fixed Mindset, where you are today is basically where you'll always be. You'll get upset when you lose, but you won't ask how you can get better.

Your mindset is your choice. I encourage you to take on the Improvement Mindset, where growth is constant, and bad days or losses are an occasion to ask how you can improve.

Part IV

6 Week Program

6 Week OSRM Program

Part IV of this book is a 6-week training schedule to get you started with improving your 40 yard dash technique, making you run the race more like an Olympic sprinter than a novice athlete.

This is where the rubber meets the road. Until now, you've primarily gained head knowledge. Head knowledge is a means to an end, not an end in itself. It is, of course, difficult to apply what you don't know. Now that you are in the know, it's time to put what you know into practice.

At the beginning of each week, review the OSRM concepts outlined for that week to ensure you're performing the drills correctly.

Note: As you apply the following 6-week program, continue your other training as usual while progressing through the six weeks. It's likely that you are working with a trainer, coach, or on a team program.

Week 1
3-Point Stance and *Visualization*

Execution

10x a day, get into your 3-point stance as if you're about to run a 40 yard dash and visualize yourself sprinting the entire race while in the stance.

Instructions

As you enter your 3-point stance, remember the three OSRMs associated with the 3-Point Stance Phase. They are 1) Hip Height, 2) Elongated Torso, and 3) Ball of the Foot.

Once in a proper 3-point stance, the Visualization should take no longer than five seconds. As you visualize, *feel* what you're visualizing. Sense it in your body, as if you're actually sprinting the entire 40 yard dash. Feel the Triple Extension, Down-and-Back, and arm action. Sense yourself driving for a solid 15 yards, transitioning for 10-15 yards, and powerfully executing the Upright Running Phase for 10-15 yards.

Week 2
3-Point Stance and *Triple Extension*

Execution
10x a day, get into your 3-point stance, then drive out for two strides, one on the left leg and one on the right leg.

Instructions
Concerning driving out, don't worry about your arms, torso, or anything else. Focus solely on the Triple Extension of each leg. As you drive off the line, keep your torso at a 45° angle in relationship to the ground.

Instructions

Just as your sole focus during a vertical leap is Triple Extension, make Triple Extension your sole focus during this week of training. Feel your legs lockout when you drive off the ground. It will seem more like bounding or jumping to you than "running."

Week 3

Triple Extension and
Up-and-Forward to Down-and-Back

Execution

10x a day, get into your 3-point stance and take two strides; one on each leg. Drive off the ground, focusing on Triple Extension and Up-and-Forward to Down-and-Back.

By now, Triple Extension will be more natural to you and not require 100% of your focus to perform. The idea with every OSRM is that you'll eventually be performing it without much, if any, conscious thought.

Instructions

In practicing your Up-and-Forward to Down-and-Back motion, imagine a water bottle is placed sideways and just in front of your feet. You need to step up-and-over the water bottle when sprinting so you don't hit it. Stride up-and-over the water bottle while simultaneously triple extending.

The reason you're simply picturing a water bottle in front of your feet is that an actual, physical water bottle may cramp your natural stride. I don't want you reaching (over striding) to make it over a physical water bottle, nor do I want you cutting your step short because you'd otherwise smash the bottle. By visualizing a water bottle in front of you with each stride, you'll naturally pick your feet up (and without the impedance of a physical object).

Week 4

Elongated Torso and
Up-and-Forward to Down-and-Back

Execution
10x a day, get into your 3-point stance and drive out for two strides; one stride each leg. As you drive out, maintain an elongated, sturdy torso, ensuring you aren't rounding or hunching your back forward.

Instructions
Many athletes, as they drive the leg either forward or back down to the ground, naturally want to "bear down." That is, they bring their chest closer to the ground because they are trying *so hard*, to the point of creating extra tension in the body. As you perform this week's OSRM training, ensure you don't bear down. The goal this week is to move your feet in an Up-and-Forward to Down-and-Back fashion while

simultaneously maintaining an Elongated Torso. To visually review this, go back to the "Asafa Powell Start" video.

Week 5
Putting It Together and *Arm Action*

Execution Part A

Pay close attention here, because this week is a bit different. 10x a day on Monday, Wednesday, and Friday, get into your 3-point stance, and perform a sprint start over 10 yards. Triple Extend with every stride, as well as move your feet in an Up-and-Forward to Down-and-Back manner. Maintain an Elongated Torso.

Instructions

Remember, a properly executed 40 yard dash start feels slightly more like bounding than running. Be patient enough to allow your legs to reach Triple Extension with each stride, then float over the ground for just a split second before powerfully punching into the ground with the ball of your foot.

Execution Part B

10x a day on Tuesday, Thursday, and Saturday, get into a 3-point stance and drive out for two strides; one on each leg. As you drive out, focus on your arms. Use powerful movements, while simultaneously keeping your face and traps loose.

Instructions

The goal of Powerful Arm Action is to counterbalance your legs. This means you'd better be swinging those arms with vigor. Again, and this point cannot be stressed enough, Powerful Arm Action does not mean tightening every muscle possible in your body. It means utilizing the muscles involved in arm swing -- chest, shoulders, and lats-- while keeping other muscles relaxed to reduce overall muscle tension in the body, thereby encouraging free-flowing limb movement.

Week 6
Evaluating Your Progress

Execution Part A

You will need a video camera this week. On Monday, Wednesday, and Friday, perform 5x20 yard sprint starts from a 3-point stance. Record them in slow-motion using either your phone, a friend's phone, or a coach's phone. If you can't record in slo-mo on your phone, be sure to plan ahead by asking someone to record your start. Between each repetition, watch the video, and *improve* upon it on your next 20 yard sprint. The 5x20 yard sprints plus the 5x watching the video will give you 10 practice opportunities, of course, utilizing both physical execution and Visualization.

Instructions

When you have completed the 6th week, choose your best slow-motion sprint start video, and email it to a friend who has also read this book for personalized feedback.

Execution Part B

10x a day on Tuesday, Thursday, and Saturday, practice Visualization. Take the best sprint start from the previous day and visualize yourself improving upon it. If your Arm Action needs work, visualize ideal arm action. If your Triple Extension needs work, visualize ideal Triple Extension, and so on.

Instructions

By no means do I expect your start to be perfect at the end of this 6-week program. I do, however, expect it to be significantly better than it was six weeks ago. If you embrace an Improvement Mindset, you will eventually embody all 11 OSRMs, resulting in freakish levels of improvement.

Warming Up and Cooling Down

A word needs to be said about warming-up and cooling down, as these popularly neglected aspects of training play a larger role in improving performance than most athletes realize.

Daily Warmup

The importance of a thorough warmup is that it prevents injury and prepares the body to create and withstand high levels of power output. To exemplify the importance of a proper warmup, consider this: If you were going to shoot a rubber band at someone, would you choose the rubber band that has been in the freezer for 12 hours, or would you choose the rubber band that was placed out in the hot sun for 15 minutes? Of course, the rubber band that was out in the sun for 15 minutes will be more elastic and spring-like than the one in the freezer. If you're training outside and it's slightly cool, extend your warmup. The rule of thumb I use with my athletes is this: Warmup until you feel as if you've run around outside in 90° heat for five minutes. When it comes to your training, don't be like the rubber band in the freezer. Again, by warming up thoroughly, your muscles will be more spring-like and less likely to snap, crackle, or pop.

Daily Cooldown

Concerning cooling down after training, always remember this equation:

Quality of Today's Workout = Quality of Yesterday's Recovery

In other words, the better you recover, the better the next day's workout will be.

Cooling down increases blood flow to the muscles. Who cares? You do. Consider this: What makes a muscle stronger? → Nutrients. What transports nutrients to your muscles? → Blood. Therefore, by increasing blood flow, you increase the nutrients transported to your muscles, which in turn promotes excellent post-workout recovery, thus better preparing you for a quality training session the following day.

Another important function of the cooldown is that it decreases your risk of injury. If your hip flexors are tight after a training session and that tightness isn't decreased by way of a cooldown, your hip flexors will stay tight for the rest of the day and throughout the night as you sleep. Tight hip flexors then result in a stressed lower back. A stressed lower back then creates tight hamstrings. As you can see, ignoring the tight hip flexors has increased your risk of straining a hamstring.

Recovery *offsets* the stress training places on your body. With that in mind, the cooldown, although it may not appear to be important on the surface, is one of the most important factors in any training program.

Final Words

The trajectory of my entire experience as an athlete was changed for the better through world-class training methods, and I'm humbled to present material in this book which, if applied, can do the same for you. If you would like to get in touch, feel free to send me an email. Before emailing, understand that I am busy and it may be a several days before you receive a response.

Want Me To Analyze Your 40 Yard Dash Start?

If you've made it this far, congratulations. As a purchaser and owner of this book, I'm offering you a discounted rate on a 40 yard dash start video analysis.

Having your start analyzed is an excellent way to improve, as I'll definitely pick up on something you hadn't noticed or thought of yourself.

To redeem this offer, you'll need to email me at nicsaluppo@gmail.com.

You'll take a slow-motion video of your 40 start from a side angle (make sure it's the side of your lead leg). Use a Google Drive link to send it. I'll analyze your start and send you feedback on two (2) specific areas. You'll then have a period of one week to implement the feedback before sending me another video. For the second video, I'll evaluate if you've successfully implemented the feedback from the first video. I'll then provide two (2) further suggestions, and that will conclude the service.

The normal rate for this service is $80.00, and I'm offering owners of this book the service for $50.00, which ends up saving you 37%.

The path is laid out before you. My hope for you and your life is that you'll choose to be the *one* and not the 999. Wishing you much success!

One Last Thing

If something in this book has been helpful to you, please take a moment to leave a review on Amazon. When you take the time to leave a review, it does not go unnoticed. It is appreciated and means a great deal to me. If you are interested in clarification of any material found in this book, feel free to send an email to nicsaluppo@gmail.com.

Made in the USA
Middletown, DE
14 December 2021